Nelson/Word Multi-Media Group
And Systems Media
Present

The Andy Griffith Show

Bible Study Series
Volume 2

Participant's Guide

Study notes written by
Joey Fann
Drew Maddux
Stephen Skelton
with
Mary Guenther,
Creative Editor

The Andy Griffith Show Bible Study Series, Volume 2
Published by Nelson Word Multi-Media Group
A division of Thomas Nelson Publishers

Copyright © 2000 by Systems Media

Printed in the United States of America
ISBN 0-8499-8833-0

For Information
Call Thomas Nelson Publishers 1-800-251-4000
www.thomasnelson.com

Introduction

What does *The Andy Griffith Show* have to do with the Bible? More than you might think.

"Christ in us" means we are being changed into His likeness. Christlikeness can be seen—in our expressions, gestures, and actions. Christlikeness can be heard—in what we say and sometimes more importantly, what we leave unsaid. Christ dwells in our laughter, our counsel, and our tears. He weaves His presence into our character as we choose to be His disciples in our everyday lives.

So come with us to Mayberry and see for yourself. Whether this is your first visit or you have been there many times, you will find joy in the journey.

About the Authors

Joey Fann is a co-instructor of the Back to Mayberry concept, the basis for *The Andy Griffith Show* Bible Study Series. He pioneered the creation of a weekly Bible class using *The Andy Griffith Show* on his website at barneyfife.com. Fann lives in Huntsville, Alabama, with his wife Nicole.

Drew Maddux is president and founder of Systems Media, LLC, a multi-media content company committed to providing entertainment for edification. By joining media and ministry, the company seeks to impact Christians in their everyday lives. Maddux lives in Nashville, Tennessee, with his wife Tara.

Stephen Skelton is director of development for Systems Media. His background includes producing for Dick Clark Productions and writing for *America's Dumbest Criminals*. He is a member of *The Andy Griffith Show* Rerun Watchers Club. Skelton lives in Nashville, Tennessee, with his wife Ashlee and daughter.

Mary Guenther, creative editor of this series, is a freelance writer and editor who lives in Nashville, Tennessee.

About Our Host

Dennis Swanberg, our host for this series, is a well-known motivational speaker, teacher, preacher, counselor and comedian. Dr. Swanberg also sketched the caricatures of Mayberry folk included in this study. His nationally broadcast television show, *Swan's Place*, is aired to over one million households. He has authored two books: *Is Your Love Tank Full?* and *Swan's Soup & Salad for Saints & Sinners*. Dr. Swanberg lives in West Monroe, Louisiana, with his wife Lauree and their sons, Dusty and Chad.

Table of Contents

NOTES

NOTES

The Andy Griffith Show
Bible Study Series
Volume 2-Session 1

"A Wife for Andy"

no

Session One
"A Wife for Andy"

"A Wife for Andy" takes a knowing look at how we sometimes take things into our own hands, rather than wait for God. As we will see, practicing patience can be easier said than done. This episode also focuses on the significance and timing of choosing a mate. Warning: Married couples should NOT save on the cost of counseling with any advice Barney gives to Andy!

Session Overview

BIBLICAL PRINCIPLE
A Parable from Mayberry

PERSONAL REFLECTION
Make Your Barney Wait

PERSONAL APPLICATION
What Would Andy Do?

ACTION POINTS
Perfecting Patience with Andy

Scriptures cited in the video include:

1. **Romans 8:25** : *But if we hope for what we do not see, we eagerly wait for it with perseverance.*
2. **Psalm 118:8:** *It is better to trust in the LORD than to put confidence in man.*
3. **James 1:4a:** *Let patience have its perfect work.*
4. **Psalm 78:19b:** *Can God prepare a table in the wilderness?*
5. **Psalm 52:9:** *I will praise You forever, Because You have done it.*

The Virtue of Patience

ROMANS 8:25
But if we hope for what we do not see, we eagerly wait for it with perseverance.

In this passage, Paul explains the importance of having hope in the things to come. While it's easy to believe in things we can see, faith is required for things we can't see (Hebrews 11:1). That is just what God calls us to do—to let go of our own understanding and put our total trust and hope in Him. If we do this, God promises that we will be richly rewarded (1 John 3:2).

BIBLICAL PRINCIPLE
A Parable from Mayberry

Even though Andy admits that being single can be downright lonesome, he has carefully considered his situation and has decided it is best to be patient and wait for the right woman, rather than focus on finding "someone." In one or two words, describe the reaction of the following characters to Andy's predicament:

Andy	
Barney	
Thelma Lou	
Helen	
Opie	
Single Ladies	

Who proved helpful to Andy? Why?

_____

_____

"See how irritable you are!"

"You know what they say about a man who keeps puttin' off gettin' married. They say he gets irritable. Yup, that's what they say...
The more he keeps puttin' it off, the more desperate he gets and the more desperate he gets, the more irritable he gets...."

"I ain't found the woman I want to marry. I ain't puttin' it off— I miss bein' married. Sometimes I feel downright lonesome. I miss goin' home to a wife. But then, you see, gettin' married means you found the woman you want to settle down with and I ain't found her yet."

Andy not only was the town sheriff, he also was a single parent trying to raise his son the best way he knew how.

How did Andy balance his responsibility to the town with his commitment to his son?

_____

_____

What qualities helped make Andy content overall as a single parent?

_____

_____

In our lives today, we tend to want everything now. Our culture of convenience rarely promotes the virtue of patience.

Do you think it would be easier to be patient in "Mayberry" than in our current culture?

_____

_____

What did Barney consider important in a wife for Andy?

_____

_____

Everyone came but Thelma Lou.

Why do you think Andy resisted Barney's help?

_____

_____

Andy does look taller.

PERSONAL REFLECTION
Make Your Barney Wait

JAMES 1:2-4

My brethren, count it all joy when you fall into various trials, knowing that the testing of your faith produces patience. But let patience have its perfect work, that you may be perfect and complete, lacking nothing.

✝ Principle: **The _____ of our faith produces**

_____.

James tells us to rejoice when we struggle because our trials produce patience. In turn, patience produces character and character produces hope—which will never disappoint us (Romans 5:3-5).

What do you think Andy learned while waiting for the right woman to appear?

_____

_____

Why do you think Andy was content to wait, rather than actively pursue marriage?

_____

_____

Surely, Helen knew what Barney wanted her to say when he probed her about her cooking and career. Why did she answer the way she did?

_____

_____

Don't you think Andy looks taller when he ain't in his uniform? Well, you do. You look taller. Miss Crump, why don't you jest stand up there next to Andy and see if he don't look taller. Go on, go on. Go on, jest stand there along side of him.... There, ya see?

Helen:

"As a matter of fact, I'm a terrible cook."

"You're just sayin' that. You're being modest...But then some day when you settle down, I mean when you get married or somethin' like that, you'll just make a terrific leg of lamb—Andy's favorite dish."

Could you do the same in similar circumstances? Why or why not?

_____

_____

Can't cook leg of lamb—Andy's favorite dish?

PERSONAL APPLICATION
What Would Andy Do?

PSALM 27:14
Wait on the LORD; Be of good courage, And He shall strengthen your heart; Wait, I say, on the LORD!

✟ Principle: **I will learn to _____ on the _____, with the Holy Spirit's help.**

Even though Barney's intentions were good, his rush to find a wife for Andy made for some "creative" matchmaking. Barney thought he could fix the situation quickly through his own wisdom. For Christians, waiting is often a time of learning in which God prepares you for what He has planned (Lamentations 3:24-26).

How often do you follow Barney's model of impatience in meeting your needs? ❑ **Never** ❑ **Rarely** ❑ **Often**
Explain.

_____

_____

Do you find it hard to admit that others might help in solving some of your problems? ❑ **Never** ❑ **Rarely** ❑ **Often**
Explain.

_____

_____

How could you best help friends through difficult situations?

_____

_____

What are the challenges of learning patience?

_____

_____

What are the rewards?

_____

_____

Credit where credit is due.

ACTION POINTS
Perfecting Patience with Andy

PSALMS 52:9
I will praise You forever, because You have done it.

The richest blessing of patience is a closer walk with God. Patience is trusting God. Rather than rely on our own meager resources, we learn to rely on Him who richly provides for us. Our attitude toward others also reflects a Christ-like acceptance, which will be our example to the world.

✝ Principle: **I will praise _____ for producing _____ in my life.**

"The sooner we get this over with the better. This dame ain't for Andy. I made a mistake... Now we cross her off our list."

Thelma Lou: "But why?"

"Because she can't cook. She can't do nothin' ...No, she's out. O-U-T, out!"

"Thanks, buddy...For last night. I really enjoyed it. Helen is one of the nicest girls I ever met...After Thelma Lou's, I walked her home and got better acquainted. Nice girl. And I owe it all to you."

Consider the following action points and plan to do at least one this week, with God's help.

I will increase my trust in God by:
- ❑ Praying daily for help to see what He is doing in my life.
- ❑ Asking Him to change my perspective on trials.
- ❑ Doing a Bible word study on "trust."

I will exercise patience by:
- ❑ Choosing to wait for God's answers to small requests, rather than take matters into my own hands.
- ❑ Asking God to give me His peace when I feel overwhelmed by circumstances.
- ❑ Asking close friends and family to pray for me to grow in patience.

I will demonstrate patience to others by:
- ❑ Listening to a friend who is struggling without giving advice.
- ❑ Taking time to understand their point of view.
- ❑ Choosing to accept, rather than judge, another's circumstances.
- ❑ Praying for a person who needs God's help to persevere in a specific trial.

A surprise for Helen.

NOTES

NOTES

The Andy Griffith Show
Bible Study Series
Volume 2-Session 2

"High Noon in Mayberry"

Session Two
"High Noon in Mayberry"

"High Noon in Mayberry" examines how we often act without knowing all the facts. This episode deals with the folly of worry and the faith it takes to trust. It also looks at the important relationship between repentance and forgiveness. Plus, Otis gets to see the world from the other side of the badge for a change.

Session Overview

BIBLICAL PRINCIPLE
A Parable from Mayberry

PERSONAL REFLECTION
The Worried Barney Within

PERSONAL APPLICATION
What Would Andy Do?

ACTION POINTS
At Ease, Like Andy

Scriptures cited in the video include:

1. **PROVERBS 29:8**
   Scoffers set a city aflame, But wise men turn away wrath.

2. **JOHN 16:33B**
   In the world you will have tribulation; but be of good cheer, I have overcome the world."

3. **PROVERBS 29:25**
   The fear of man brings a snare, But whoever trusts in the LORD shall be safe.

4. **PROVERBS 16:3**
   Commit your works to the LORD, And your thoughts will be established.

5. **PSALM 56:9**
   When I cry out to You, Then my enemies will turn back; This I know, because God is for me.

6. **ZECHARIAH 4:6B**
   "Not by might nor by power, but by My Spirit," Says the LORD of hosts.

Worry is a Waste

LUKE 12:25-26

And which of you by worrying can add one cubit to his stature? If you then are not able to do the least, why are you anxious for the rest?

In this passage, Jesus tells his disciples not to worry. Worrying is futile and God knows exactly what we need. Instead of worrying, we should focus our energy on God, who has promised to provide for our needs. If we put our faith in Him, He will provide us an eternal perspective! Faith alone can free us from worry.

BIBLICAL PRINCIPLE
A Parable from Mayberry

Andy has received a disturbing letter. Several years ago, Andy had wounded Luke Comstock during a robbery gunfight. And now, Luke is coming back to Mayberry to "set things straight." Consider the following characters and use one or two words to describe their reaction to Andy's situation.

Andy	
Barney	
Otis	
Gomer	
Opie	
Aunt Bee	

Which character most closely matches your own initial reaction? Why?

_____

_____

The call of duty.

"Now, you listen to me and you listen good. Everything about that letter— the way it's written, the way it's folded, the way the envelope is sealed— everything about it says just one thing: R-E-V-E-N-G!"

Living on this planet provides ample opportunities to worry. Almost daily, we deal with situations with an uncertain outcome. And sometimes the initial prognosis doesn't look good! Andy received some news that he probably didn't want to hear. Yet, his reaction was measured. Despite Barney's concerns, Andy resisted the urge to worry.

Was Barney's reaction to the letter totally irrational?
❑ **Yes**   ❑ **No**   ❑ **Maybe**   *Explain.*

_____

_____

Do you think Andy should have taken more precautions to protect himself?   ❑ **Yes**   ❑ **No**
Why do you think he chose not to?

_____

_____

A "plain-clothes" operation.

Despite their bumbling, were you relieved when Barney and his "deputies" planned to stake out Andy's house?   ❑ **Yes**   ❑ **No**
Why or why not?

_____

_____

How do you think Andy's admission of fear following Luke's call affected Opie? Aunt Bee?

_____

_____

Luke is on his way.

PERSONAL REFLECTION
The Worried Barney Within

PROVERBS 3:5-6
Trust in the LORD with all your heart, And lean not on your own understanding; In all your ways acknowledge Him, And He shall direct your paths.

✝ Principle: **I will trust the _____ to _____ the way.**

Barney automatically assumed the worst. Likewise, instead of trusting that God will take care of us, we often believe we must control the unknown—as if we could! However, if we put our trust in Him, He promises to show us the way. When we make Him a part of all we do, He will guide us because we will be working to accomplish His will (Matthew 6:33).

Put yourself in Andy's place. How would you react to receiving such a letter? What does your answer reveal about your inclination to worry?

_____

_____

Why do you think Andy decided to put his gun back on the shelf, rather than load it before Luke came?

_____

_____

Would you have taken the same chance? Why or why not?

_____

_____

"Are you scared, Pa?"

"Well, I am a little nervous."

Opie:
"Is this your first time?"

Andy:
"No, I've been scared a whole lot of times."

Opie:
"Really, Pa? Gosh, you sure couldn't tell it."

Luke:

"I had a chance to review my whole life— when I was a boy to where I was lying with my leg game for life. All I could think was what a waste. So I made up my mind then and there. I was going to make something out of myself, Sheriff. I began reading and studying while I was still in the hospital...If you hadn't laid me up, who knows where I'd be today."

MARK 4:35-41

On the same day, when evening had come, He said to them, "Let us cross over to the other side." Now when they had left the multitude, they took Him along in the boat as He was. And other little boats were also with Him. And a great windstorm arose, and the waves beat into the boat, so that it was already filling. But He was in the stern, asleep on a pillow. And they awoke Him and said to Him, "Teacher, do You not care that we are perishing?" Then He arose and rebuked the wind, and said to the sea, "Peace, be still!" And the wind ceased and there was a great calm. But He said to them, "Why are you so fearful? How is it that you have no faith?" And they feared exceedingly, and said to one another, "Who can this be, that even the wind and the sea obey Him!"

Picture the disciples in a boat that is full of water on a stormy sea. Did they have cause to worry? Yet, Jesus rebuked them for their lack of faith.

The same Jesus that was with them in the boat is with us—every minute of every day. He still has the same power to quiet the storm. Yet, we worry instead.

Note that Jesus did not say that a little bit of worrying was okay. *No* worry. That's our goal. How can we possibly do that?

✝ Principle: **My _____ comes from the _____ who strengthens me.**

What are some advantages of putting our lives in the hands of the Lord?

_____

_____

How important was it for Luke to forgive Andy?

_____

_____

Otis' worst nightmare.

PSALM 56:3
Whenever I am afraid, I will trust in You.

Fear often drives us to worry, rather than to the Lord. As Christians, we can even pray "worried prayers." For example, we pray, *"Lord, please don't let anything bad happen to my children at school today"* rather than, *"Thank You, Lord, for Your eternal love for us. I place my children in Your watchful care today."*

As you notice, the first prayer focuses on the potential dangers a child may face. The second prayer focuses on the goodness of God and trusting Him with our children.

Why is it important to focus on God, rather than our own concerns?
_____
_____

What area in your life causes you the most anxiety?
_____
_____

What is a good way to pray about this area? (See Philippians 4:6-7 below.)
_____
_____

The posse arrives.

ACTION POINTS
At Ease Like Andy

PHILIPPIANS 4:6-7
Be anxious for nothing, but in everything by prayer and supplication, with thanksgiving, let your requests be made known to God, and the peace of God, which surpasses all understanding, will guard your hearts and minds through Christ Jesus.

"Okay, Okay. So how was I to know? I can't read people's minds. Comstock is an ex-con and I took it from there."

"Barney, we talked about it all last night and all this morning. As far as I'm concerned, the whole matter is closed. No harm done."

Otis:

"Listen, I'm sure sorry about last night. I didn't want to be a deputy anyway. Well, it's all Barney's fault. He..."

"We agreed not to talk about it anymore."

Otis:

"Oh, I see. Tick-a-lock?"

"Tick-a-lock."

✝ **I can surrender my _____ to Jesus and take His _____ instead.**

Have you ever noticed that most of the things we worry about never come to pass? Rather, it is things that we *don't* see coming that often cause problems. Nevertheless, God will take care of us in every circumstance.

Worry will not disappear quickly for most of us. Andy learned to trust over time and through many experiences. It will be the same for us. In time, we can replace the habit of worry with a habit of turning to God for His assurance.

Consider the following action points and plan to do at least one of them this week, with God's help.

I will lean on the Lord instead of myself by:
❑ Daily writing down everything I think I need to worry about and offering these concerns to God instead *(e.g., burn it, shred it; wad it up, etc.).*
❑ Trusting that God will work in all of the above issues;
❑ Reading His Word and listening to His Spirit.

I will grow in faith by:
❑ Focusing on the goodness of God;
❑ Choosing to believe that God is in control—especially when I am not;
❑ Completing a Bible word study on "worry" and "anxiety."

I will develop the courage to face life's challenges by:
❑ Asking God for help;
❑ Facing a specific fear head on, rather than trying to avoid or deny it;
❑ Drawing strength from the prayers and counsel of mature Christian friends.

All's well that ends well

NOTES

NOTES

The Andy Griffith Show
Bible Study Series
Volume 2-Session 3

"Barney's First Car"

Session Three
"Barney's First Car"

"Barney's First Car" shows how our material wants can blind our better judgment. This episode points out the pitfalls of rash actions and foolish pride. It also demonstrates that dishonesty can be detected with wisdom. And you'll be glad Barney's bullet isn't in the barrel, when you see his fast reflex to a good deal!

Session Overview

BIBLICAL PRINCIPLE
A Parable from Mayberry

PERSONAL REFLECTION
Wiser than Barney

PERSONAL APPLICATION
What Would Andy Do?

ACTION POINTS
Pursuing Prudence Like Andy

Scriptures cited in the video include:

1. **ECCLESIASTES 9:17B**
   Words of the wise, spoken quietly, should be heard.

2. **PROVERBS 14:15**
   The simple believes every word, But the prudent man considers well his steps.

3. **PROVERBS 18:15**
   The heart of the prudent acquires knowledge,

4. **PROVERBS 1:10**
   My son, if sinners entice you, Do not consent.

5. **JOB 34:3**
   For the ear tests words As the palate tastes food.

PROVERBS 15:22
Without counsel, plans go awry, But in the multitude of counselors they are established.

Prudence is a rather old-fashioned word for a timeless virtue. It means applying skill and good judgment in the use of resources. We learn prudence over time, with experience and good counsel. When we are short on experience, we should be *long* on counsel. None of us can afford to make important decisions based on convenience, laziness, or "feeling good" about something—as Barney found out almost too late.

BIBLICAL PRINCIPLE
A Parable from Mayberry

Barney was quite anxious to buy his first car. Although he had plenty of enthusiasm, he seemed to lack wisdom. In one or two words, describe the reaction of the following characters to Barney's inexperienced decision:

Barney	
Andy	
Mrs. Lesh	
Gomer	
Thelma Lou	
Aunt Bee	
Opie	

Whom would you choose from the above list as your model? Why?

_____

_____

Love at first sight.

"Tomorrow's Sunday. Why don't you wait 'til the first of the week before you make such a big decision?"

"Ange, when the old steel trap in here has made up its mind, there's no turning back."

Barney's approach to buying a car is not uncommon. Sometimes we think we know what we want, so we act—without considering the consequences. Unfortunately, this approach leaves God out of the decision-making process. Mercifully, God does not desert us in our ignorance, and Barney would learn a lot from his mistake!

Mrs. Lesh (aka "Myrt") milks her audience.

Barney justified his actions by telling Andy, "I'm going to live a little." It's easy to rationalize our decisions by saying that we deserve it.

Do you think there is anything wrong with this kind of attitude?
❑ **Yes**　　❑ **No**
Why or why not?

_____

_____

Why do you think Barney ignored Andy's advice?

_____

_____

At what point do you think Barney realized he had made a mistake?

_____

_____

Why was Andy able to see the potential pitfalls of car-buying more clearly than Barney?

_____

_____

PROVERBS 14:15
The simple believes every word, but the prudent man considers well his steps.

✟ Principle: **We must _____ before we _____.**

Barney was more than willing to risk all he had to buy the car. When Andy cautioned him, Barney plainly wasn't interested. It's easy to decide what we're going to do with our resources and *then* ask God's blessing on *our* decision.

What are some dangers of going with your "gut feeling"?

_____

_____

Though Barney did not heed his advice, Andy didn't abandon Barney, laugh at him, or say, "I told you so." He stuck by his friend and helped him resolve the situation.

Could you have been as supportive under similar circumstances?
❑ **Yes**   ❑ **No**   ❑ **Maybe**

_____

_____

Three hundred easy clams.

"Don't you think you're jumpin' into this thing awful fast? ...Now I'd advise you to take a spin in it. Go over to the fillin' station and have Wally crawl around underneath and look it over."

"It wouldn't be an insult. Now, this is business. It's a big step in your life."

Jake:

"How'd you do, Myrt?"

Mrs. Lesh:

"I unloaded another one, Jake. Three hundred easy clams from the sucker of the world."

Too much grease in the steering column?

PERSONAL APPLICATION
Persuing Prudence Like Andy

PROVERBS 19:20
Listen to counsel and receive instruction, That you may be wise in your latter days.

✝ Principle: **We must _____ to obtain _____. Prudence is one _____ of wisdom.**

While Andy encouraged careful consideration, emotion drove Barney. In each case, their actions were a reflection of their prudence and wisdom. Prudence is a rational act. To obtain it, we should heed the advice of people who manage their own resources wisely. Most importantly, we should always seek the will of God in all that we do.

Think of someone whom you consider wise and prudent. Do they believe they always have the right answer? ☐ **Yes** ☐ **No**
What does that tell you about gaining wisdom?

_____

_____

When the car didn't live up to Barney's expectation, he could hardly believe it. Instead of taking responsibility for his actions, Barney felt sorry for himself.

We all at times have blamed others or felt sorry for ourselves when a decision we made turned out poorly.

What are some positive things we can learn from such mistakes?

_____

_____

Deceitful people often appeal to our emotions to convince us to do things we would not otherwise do—especially with our money.

How could prudence protect you from this kind of exploitation?

_____

_____

Mayberry or bust!

ACTION POINTS
Pursuing Prudence

PROVERBS 2:10-13
When wisdom enters your heart, And knowledge is pleasant to your soul, Discretion will preserve you; Understanding will keep you, To deliver you from the way of evil, From the man who speaks perverse things, From those who leave the paths of uprightness To walk in the ways of darkness.

We make decisions every day. Some decisions are small and have little consequence, while others are very important and may affect the rest of our lives. In either event, we should prayerfully consider the decision and consult with others for objective guidance. Recognize the will of God and trust that He has a plan for you.

✝ Principle: **I will look to _____ for _____.**

Myrt:

"Let me make a deal with ya. You forget what happened, and I'll let you have a sweet 1958 custom sedan that's been in the garage— up on blocks— since 1959."

"That sounds like what I've been lookin' for!"

"Well, now I got my money back, I'm gonna be a little more careful.
...I've learned my lesson. Trust nobody.
...You can fool Barney Fife once, maybe— just once!— but never again."

Consider the following action points and plan to do at least one of them this week, with God's help.

I will carefully consider an important decision by:
- ❑ Spending time in prayer;
- ❑ Researching the available facts;
- ❑ Seeking the advice of someone wiser than myself.

I will exercise prudence by:
- ❑ Taking an inventory of my time, energy, and financial resources;
- ❑ Asking God to show me His priorities for their use;
- ❑ Developing a personal schedule and/or budget to focus on God's priorities.

I will consider others by:
- ❑ Sharing what I have learned about prudence with a family member or friend;
- ❑ Giving up one of my wants to provide someone else's need;
- ❑ Giving counsel to someone who has asked me for it.

Myrt's gang brings her another car.

NOTES

NOTES

The Andy Griffith Show
Bible Study Series
Volume 2-Session 4

"The Great Filling Station Robbery"

Session Four
"The Great Filling Station Robbery"

"The Great Filling Station Robbery" shows that a suspicious mind jumps to a convenient conclusion. This episode addresses the connection between character and accusation. It also illustrates that deception can be countered with wisdom. And notice how, with a simple faith, Gomer disregards rumors, paying them very little mind—because that's all he can afford!

Session Overview

BIBLICAL PRINCIPLE
A Parable from Mayberry

PERSONAL REFLECTION
Building a Better Barney

PERSONAL APPLICATION
What Would Andy Do?

ACTION POINTS
Trust Like Andy

Scriptures cited in the video include:

1. **ISAIAH 55:8**
   "For My thoughts are not your thoughts, Nor are your ways My ways," says the LORD.

2. **PROVERBS 11:9**
   The hypocrite with his mouth destroys his neighbor.

3. **JAMES 1:19**
   So then, my beloved brethren, let every man be swift to hear, slow to speak, slow to wrath.

4. **1 CORINTHIANS 13:6**
   [Love] does not rejoice in iniquity, but rejoices in the truth.

5. **ROMANS 12:14**
   Bless those who persecute you; bless and do not curse.

6. **ROMANS 12:17**
   Repay no one evil for evil. Have regard for good things in the sight of all men.

1 CORINTHIANS 13:6
[Love] does not delight in iniquity, but rejoices in the truth.

The search for truth is not always an easy task. Often, it takes careful deliberation to thoroughly assess a person or an event. A person's reputation is fragile. Thus, the search for truth requires the right attitude—love. The scripture above reminds us that love does not take pleasure in what is wrong, but celebrates what is right.

BIBLICAL PRINCIPLE
A Parable from Mayberry

While filling station owner Wally is out of town, things turn up missing. The evidence seems to point to a young man named Jimmy Morgan. Consider the following characters and use one or two words to describe their opinion of Jimmy.

Mr. Carter	
Barney	
Gomer	
Andy	

What was your initial reaction to Jimmy? Did you prove to be correct?

_____

_____

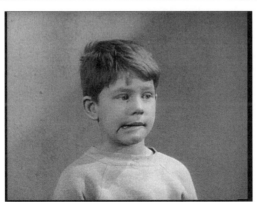
"Lefty" plots his breakout.

"It's an inner-com. Just what this place has been needing. It's about time we started modernizin' this place electronally..."

"This is the age of science know-how, electronal marvels."

Mr. Carter:

"I finally found who stole the battery out of my truck. Just as I figured all along, it was young Morgan here. You know, I hired him to make deliveries for me. I paid him a sight more than he was worth. And just the minute my back was turned, he stole me blind. Well, he certainly did."

On your car?

It can be difficult to believe in someone, especially in the face of others' harsh assessments. We are tempted to judge others on superficial appearance, and when we look without love, we become critical.

Even when Andy could have passed judgment based on circumstance, he kept choosing to give Jimmy another chance. In the end, Jimmy proved Andy right.

Why do you think Mr. Carter accused Jimmy of stealing his battery?

_____

_____

Did Andy have much reason to trust Jimmy?

_____

_____

Why did he give Jimmy so many chances to prove himself?

_____

_____

Why do you suppose the Hanson brothers chose the week Wally was gone to pull off their heist? Is there such a thing as being too trusting?

_____

_____

To this point in his life, do you think many people had trusted Jimmy?
❑ **Yes**   ❑ **No**   ❑ **No opinion**   *Explain your answer.*

_____

_____

PERSONAL REFLECTION
Finding the Barney Within

PROVERBS 11:9
The hypocrite with his mouth destroys his neighbor,
But through knowledge the righteous will be delivered.

✝ Principle: **We should not _____ about another person without _____ all the facts.**

While Andy was concerned about Jimmy as an individual, Barney was more concerned with the latest in criminal detection technology. In his pursuit, Barney lost sight of the human aspect. Although he appeared to be gathering facts, actually he had already made his judgment. In doing so, Barney ignored the most important piece of evidence—Jimmy's heart.

Did you find yourself believing that Jimmy was guilty as the evidence continued to pile up against him? ☐ **Yes** ☐ **No**
Why or why not?

_____

_____

Jimmy loses his job with Mr. Carter.

In your opinion, what did Mr. Carter mean when he said that he didn't want "a boy like Jimmy" working for him anymore?

_____

_____

Mr. Carter:

"Oh, and this, this was your idea, Sheriff. 'Give him a chance,' you said. 'He's always gettin' in trouble, so give him a job, and let him prove what he can do.' Well he certainly proved it!"

"I don't know why you didn't just bring him in. It seems like an open and shut case to me."

People with a "past" are more likely to cause trouble than others.
☐ **True**   ☐ **False**   *Explain your answer.*

_____

_____

Have you ever given up on someone who needed your trust?

_____

_____

Like Gomer, have you ever been burned by someone you trusted? .
☐ **Yes**   ☐ **No**
If so, how has it affected your ability to trust others?

_____

_____

PERSONAL APPLICATION
Building a Better Barney

ROMANS 12:16-18
Be of the same mind toward one another. Do not set your mind on high things, but associate with the humble. Do not be wise in your own opinion. Repay no one evil for evil. Have regard for good things in the sight of all men. If it is possible, as much as depends on you, live peaceably with all men.

✝ Principle: **We are called to _____ ourselves and see the _____ in others.**

The set-up seems too obvious.

Usually, our first reaction is to strike back when we have been wronged. But when we love others as Jesus loves us, we are willing to forgive instead (Matthew 5:38-42). To Jimmy Morgan, it seemed everyone was against him. Yet, rather than strike back or give up, he focused on showing others the good inside himself without putting anyone else down. Jimmy had faith that the truth would prevail.

Put yourself in Jimmy's place. How would you react if someone unjustly accused you?

_____

_____

As you compare the attitudes of Andy and Mr. Carter, what can you learn about the way you treat others?

_____

_____

Not a soul in sight.

ACTION POINTS
Pursuing Prudence

JOHN 7:24
Do not judge according to appearance, but judge with righteous judgment.

✝ Principle: **I will seek the _____ before forming an _____.**

Let's face it, we're all human and we can let each other down. As the Apostle Paul wrote to the Romans, "*We have all sinned and fallen short of the glory of God*" (Romans 3:23).

"Now the trap is set. Gomer, from now on, anyone entering these premises, the minute he opens this door, he triggers that apparatus and gets his picture took."

Gomer:

"Sha-zamm! Captain Marvel wouldn't of thought of that, Barney."

"I guess we'll have to chalk one up to the youth of today, Barn—not to mention good old scientific know-how."

Nevertheless, we shouldn't let past failures drag us down or cause us to needlessly attack our brother or sister. We can ask God for the compassion to give them a second chance. Instead of either being naïve or rushing to judgment, we ought to rush to listen—and pray—so that we are able to make a *right* judgment.

Consider the following action points and plan to do at least one of them this week, with God's help.

I will increase my trust in others by asking God to:
- ❑ Heal me of hurts from the past involving trust;
- ❑ Surface any hidden prejudice in me;
- ❑ Help me look past the external and into the heart of others.

I will seek to become a better listener by:
- ❑ Taking time to listen to someone with whom I disagree, setting aside and not voicing my own opinion *(this should be a friend, family member, spouse, or co-worker)*;
- ❑ In "spirited" discussions at work, I will concentrate on what someone else is saying, rather than on my own response;
- ❑ Taking notes during the Sunday sermons.

I will grow in my ability to look past appearances by:
- ❑ Spending 2-3 hours people-watching in an airport, library, or similar place with many people, asking God to show me how He sees individuals that I find "unusual";
- ❑ Reaching out and befriending someone that I have previously avoided because of the way they look;
- ❑ Asking God to bring me some "surprising" friends.

The wonders of science.

NOTES

NOTES

OTHER EZ LESSON PLANS

The EZ Lesson Plan was designed with the facilitator in mind. This new format gives you the flexibility as a teacher to use the video as the visual and then refer to the facilitator's guide for the questions…and even better, the answers. It is designed for a four-week study, communicated by our top authors and it is totally self-contained. **Each EZ Lesson Plan requires the student's guides to be purchased separately as we have maintained a very low purchase price on the video resource.**

Please visit your local Christian bookstore to see the other titles we have available in the EZ Lesson Plan format. We have listed some of the titles and authors for your convenience:

EZ LESSON PLANS NOW AVAILABLE:

The 10 Commandments of Dating   **Ben Young and Dr. Samuel Adams**
AVAILABLE NOW

Are you tired of pouring time, energy, and money into relationships that start off great and end with heartache? If so, you need *The 10 Commandments of Dating* to give you the hard-hitting, black-and-white, practical guidelines that will address your questions and frustrations about dating. This guide will help you keep your head in the search for the desire of your heart.
EZ Lesson Plan ISBN: 0-7852-9619-0   **Student's Guide ISBN: 0-7852-9621-2**

Extreme Evil: Kids Killing Kids   **Bob Larson**
AVAILABLE NOW

Kids are killing kids in public schools! Kids are killing their parents! What is causing all of this evil in our younger generation? Do we need prayer back in the schools…or do we need God to start in the home? Bob Larson gets us to the root of these evils and brings us some of the answers we are looking for in this new video assisted program.
EZ Lesson Plan ISBN: 0-7852-9701-4   **Student's Guide ISBN: 0-7852-9702-2**

Life Is Tough, but God Is Faithful   **Sheila Walsh**
AVAILABLE NOW

Sheila takes a look at eight crucial turning points that can help you rediscover God's love and forgiveness. Showing how the choices you make affect your life, she offers insights from the book of Job, from her own life, and from the lives of people whose simple but determined faith helped them become shining lights in a dark world.
EZ Lesson Plan ISBN: 0-7852-9618-2   **Student's Guide ISBN: 0-7852-9620-4**

Why I Believe   **D. James Kennedy**
AVAILABLE NOW

In this video, Dr. D. James Kennedy offers intelligent, informed responses to frequently heard objections to the Christian faith. By dealing with topics such as the Bible, Creation, the Resurrection and the return of Christ, *Why I Believe* provides a solid foundation for Christians to clarify their own thinking while becoming more articulate in the defense of their faith.
EZ Lesson Plan ISBN: 0-7852-8770-9   **Student's Guide ISBN: 0-7852-8769-5**

The Lord's Prayer   **Jack Hayford**
AVAILABLE NOW

Why do we say "Thy Kingdom come?" What does "Hallowed be Thy Name" mean? Do we really practice "Forgive us our debts as we forgive our debtors?" Pastor Jack Hayford walks you through verse-by-verse and then applies this great scripture to our personal lives. This study will put "meaning to the words" you have just been saying for years.

EZ Lesson Plan ISBN: 0-7852-9442-2   **Student's Guide ISBN: 0-7852-9609-3**

How to Pray   **Ronnie Floyd**
AVAILABLE NOW

Whether you are a rookie in prayer or a seasoned prayer warrior, this video kit will meet you where you are and take you to another level in your prayer life. You may have been raised in a Christian home where prayer was a normal, daily exercise. You may have attended church all of your life, where the prayers of the people and the minister were as common as the hymns that still ring in your ears. Yet such experiences do not guarantee that you know how to pray. With simple, yet profound prose, Dr. Floyd declares, "prayer occurs when you depend on God, prayerlessness occurs when you depend on yourself."

EZ Lesson Plan ISBN: 0-8499-8790-3   **Student's Guide ISBN: 0-8499-8793-8**

Healing Prayer   **Reginald Cherry, M.D.**
AVAILABLE NOW

"Prayer is the divine key that unlocks God's pathway to healing in both the natural and supernatural realms of life." In Healing Prayer, Dr. Cherry explores the connection between faith and healing, the Bible and medicine. He blends the latest research, true stories, and biblical principles to show that spirit-directed prayers can bring healing for disease.

EZ Lesson Plan ISBN: 0-7852-9666-2   **Student's Guide ISBN: 0-7852-9667-0**

Jesus and The Terminator   **Jack Hayford**
AVAILABLE NOW

From the **E-Quake** Series comes the EZ Lesson Plan that is the focal point of the book of Revelation. Pastor Hayford sets the stage for the fight against the Evil One when the end of time comes upon us. There is no greater force than that of Jesus, and now viewers will see Him become triumphant again in this battle that is evident.

EZ Lesson Plan ISBN: 0-7852-9601-8   **Student's Guide ISBN: 0-7852-9658-1**

The Law of Process   **John C. Maxwell**
AVAILABLE NOW

Leadership develops daily, not in a day. This law, taken from **The Twenty One Irrefutable Laws of Leadership** is the first of the series to be placed into an individual study. Take each opportunity as it comes along and find the answer in a way only strong leaders would do it…by processing it. John explains how and why "Champions don't become champions in the ring…they are merely recognized there."

EZ Lesson Plan ISBN: 0-7852-9671-9   **Student's Guide ISBN: 0-7852-9672-7**

Forgiveness   John MacArthur
AVAILABLE NOW

In this three-session EZ Lesson Plan, noted biblical scholar John MacArthur provides an insightful look at forgiveness. MacArthur not only reminds us that we are called to grant forgiveness to those who sin against us, but he also teaches the importance of learning to accept the forgiveness of others.

EZ Lesson Plan ISBN: 0-8499-8808-X   **Student's Guide ISBN: 0-8499-8809-8**

Andy Griffith Volume 1 Bible Study Series   Systems Media, Inc.
AVAILABLE NOW

For generations, stories have been used to teach universal truths. In keeping with this time-honored tradition, the new three-volume *Andy Griffith Bible Study Series* has been developed, which uses the classic stories of Mayberry to illustrate biblical truths. In *Honesty*, the first volume of the series, learn from Andy, Opie, and the gang as they struggle with, and learn from, everyday life situations.

EZ Lesson Plan ISBN: 0-8499-8815-2   **Student's Guide ISBN: 0-8499-8816-0**

Created to Be God's Friend   Henry Blackaby
AVAILABLE NOW

Henry Blackaby, called to be a pastor and living his life as a man of God, teaches us how all of us are created equal in being God's friend. No Christian need live without a keen sense of purpose, and no believer need give up on finding daily closeness with God.

EZ Lesson Plan ISBN: 0-7852-9718-9   **Student's Guide ISBN: 0-7852-6758-1**

EZ LESSON PLANS COMING SOON:

The Murder of Jesus   John MacArthur
AVAILABLE AUGUST 22, 2000

To many, the story of Christ's crucifixion has become so familiar that it has lost its ability to shock, outrage or stir any great emotion. In *The Murder of Jesus*, John MacArthur presents this pivotal moment in the life of Jesus in a way that forces the viewers to witness this event in all its power. The passion of Christ is examined chronologically through the lens of the New Testament with special attention given to Jesus' words on the cross, the miracles that attended the crucifixion, and the significance of Christ's atoning work.

EZ Lesson Plan ISBN: 0-8499-8796-2   **Student's Guide ISBN: 0-8499-8797-0**

Fresh Brewed Life   Nicole Johnson
AVAILABLE SEPTEMBER 5, 2000

God is calling us to wake up, to shout an enthusiastic "Yes" to life, just as we say "Yes" to our first cup of coffee each morning. Nothing would please Him more than for us to live fresh-brewed lives steeped with His love, filling the world with the marvelous aroma of Christ. The EZ Lesson Plan will provide humor, vignettes, and in-depth study to small groups on this topic.

EZ Lesson Plan ISBN: 0-7852-9723-5   **Student's Guide ISBN: 0-7852-9724-3**

The Law of Respect   **John C. Maxwell**
AVAILABLE JULY 25, 2000

We are taught from our parents to respect others. Our business practices are to be ones of respecting others' ideas, thoughts, and mainly their motivations. We tend to get caught up in the daily routines, but if we do not respect those around us and the ones we work with, our success will be held at a low ebb. John Maxwell is a leader's leader.

EZ Lesson Plan ISBN: 0-7852-9756-1   **Student's Guide ISBN: 0-7852-9757-X**

Becoming a Woman of Grace   **Cynthia Heald**
AVAILABLE SEPTEMBER 1, 2000

This is a newly formatted product built around a message that only Cynthia Heald could deliver to us. Women have proven to be the stronger of the sexes in prayer, empathy, and faith. Cynthia leads this women's group study on how a woman can become A Woman of Grace through prayer, obedience to God and other practices of their lives. This EZ Lesson Plan will bring the components of this publishing product to one, self-contained format ready to start small groups.

EZ Lesson Plan ISBN: 0-7852-9706-5   **Student's Guide ISBN: 0-7852-9707-3**

Andy Griffith Volume 2 Bible Study Series   **Systems Media**
AVAILABLE SEPTEMBER 12, 2000

In the Andy Griffith Volume 2 Bible Study Series you will see four great studies: First lesson: "A Wife for Andy" teaches us about integrity in looking for a spouse, as well as in handling friends a bit over-eager to see their plans to help us succeed—even if it kills us! Second lesson: "High Noon in Mayberry" illustrates the futility of worry, both in mind and in action. When Andy decides not to assume the worst, he is able to relax and enjoy the true intent of his former enemy's visit. Not so, for the posse outside his door! Third lesson: "Barney's First Car" is a roller-coaster ride of elation, dejection, amazement, and deception as Barney's friends loyally support him through his crisis. Fourth lesson: "The Great Filling Station Robbery" demonstrates the damage we can do to others' reputations when our perceptions do not keep pace with their growth.

EZ Lesson Plan ISBN: 0-8499-8832-2   **Student's Guide ISBN: 0-8499-8833-0**